HUE COLORING

50 BEAUTIFUL BIRD DESIGNS

An Adult Coloring Book

ISBN-13: 978-1523757671
ISBN-10: 1523757671

IN THIS COLORING BOOK...

50 beautiful bird designs are included in this adult coloring book to help you relax and make your life more colorful. These illustrations are created for you to bring enjoyment to your life, and designed with beautiful patterns that appeal to adult eyes.

TIPS TO A FUN COLORING

Find a quiet space. It's easier to focus on what you are doing when there are no distractions.

Organize your materials. Lay out your coloring book and crayons, pens, or pencils.

Set the mood. Turn on some tranquil music, diffuse lavender or another relaxing oil, and make sure you have your preferred drink at hand.

Select your picture. Which image speaks to you today? That's the one you should color. Choose your palette. Select the colors you will be using for your image.

Begin coloring. This is the fun part. Don't worry about getting everything perfect; just start. If you feel you don't want to do it anymore, just stop!

SHOW US YOUR CREATION!

We'd love to hear from you, show us what you created.
Facebook: www.facebook.com/huecoloring
Pinterest: www.pinterest.com/huecoloring

Please be sure to subscribe to our newsletter by visiting: huecoloring.com. We'll show you our latest coloring projects as well as giving you information of the best deals.

Sources Images: Credit to geraria, Cat_arch_angel, pinterest.com, mastapiece, ArtMari, MiaMilky, pixhder,DiviVector, Evgeniia Zagreeva, abyssus cruor, Alsou Shakurova, Alexander_P, mika cha, rudall30 maverick10191, renikca, dragoart, sonkes, vitasunny, Mishka Sem, alrynnas, golubok, MaKars,sonkes, Viktoriyaa, mart, alrynnas, pinterest, Natali Snailcat, Merggy, freepik.com, Danussa
Alexander_P, Aric Chong, diana pryadieva, alrynnas, Natsmith, NEILRAS, mastapiece, OK-SANA, OK-SANA, Potapov Alexander, Nattle, Natali Snailcat, Megapixelina, KostanPROFF, daver2002ua,
Anna Paff, Olga Korneeva, Yulia Tashirova, Anna Paff, mastapiece, Adam Fahey Designs, TorriPhoto, Irina Voloshina from Shutterstocks.

SHOW US YOUR CREATION!

We'd love to hear from you, show us what you created.
Facebook: www.facebook.com/huecoloring
Pinterest: www.pinterest.com/huecoloring

Please be sure to subscribe to our newsletter by visiting: huecoloring.com. We'll show you our latest coloring projects as well as giving you information of the best deals.

www.ingramcontent.com/pod-product-compliance
Lightning Source LLC
Chambersburg PA
CBHW081359280526
45788CB00009B/2930